Unknowne Land

Eléna Rivera

THE FRANCES JAFFER BOOK AWARD

KELSEY ST. PRESS

FOR RUSSELL

I am grateful to the editors of *Rooms, Volt, Apex of the M* and
Salt Hill, in which sections of *Unknowne Land* first appeared.
I would also like to acknowledge the Millay Colony where
one of the sections of this poem was written.

This award for the publication of a first book honors the memory
of Bay Area poet, editor and feminist Frances Jaffer, 1921–1999.

Judge: Kathleen Fraser

Library of Congress Cataloging-in-Publication Data

Rivera, Eléna
    Unknowne Land / Eléna Rivera
        p. cm.
    "The Francis Jaffer Book Award."
    ISBN 0-932716-53-9 (alk. paper)
        I. Title.

    PS3568.I8292 U55 2000
    811'.6–dc21

                                        00-027384

Series design by Poulson/Gluck Design

All orders to: Small Press Distribution
                  800-869-7553   email: orders@spdbooks.org

Please note: We do not read unsolicited manuscripts for this award.

You can visit Kelsey St. Press online at: www.kelseyst.com

CONTENTS

FIRE

7

EARTH

13

WATER

25

AIR

35

THE SPHERE

45

Unknowne
Land

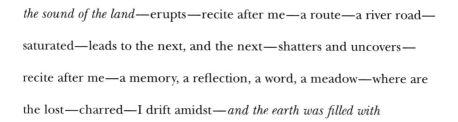

the sound of the land—erupts—recite after me—a route—a river road—
saturated—leads to the next, and the next—shatters and uncovers—
recite after me—a memory, a reflection, a word, a meadow—where are
the lost—charred—I drift amidst—*and the earth was filled with*

FIRE

Who bears a record of the world?

Exploding.   At the beginning   there

were no witnesses, and now   we are under

the weight of illumination.

Glowing embers

yield up so much.

The figure leans forward.

I am that figure, elbow

down on the desk, full

of North wind; a figure

shown, shorn, fastened

to too many voices.

a burnt child dreads the fire

Behind the framework

a body retreats   and then

again   catapulted forward—

into a lament, pulled into

the rhythm of the pencil

as it adheres to the page, in

the quivering cold wind,

fastening the flame to the glass.

What to do with a red child,

scribbled on a piece of paper?

In the interval, between childhood

and when the figure was clothed.

The moment midway (putting

on the bra), halfway (pulling up

the underwear), between being nude

and clothed. A private space

set burning. Closed and nude.

where there is much light

the shadows are deepest

Between what you need

and what she needs   (intense,

turbulent, furious, destructive).

I step into the room. I am stepping

into, step in. Ruins at the border.

I follow the glimpse, the 'almost.'

Scarlet, rubiate, sanguine, carmine.

not as honest with myself as I

Simulate a tale, a way out

of the cinders (where she was

headed), full of expectations,

in her superimposed box.

She puts on her uniform,

white shirt, gray skirt,

dark blue pullover.

a torn limb held out toward the sun

She speaks in another language.

I confused her movements with

the space around her. I tried to

follow her, an intervention of the

alternate line; I tried to live her

secrets, her fantasy, even though

it came hard   (hearing).

Created! Gleaming! Glowing!

the liberating scream

Captive. She finds her notes

are connected by a bind. She

hovers over the debris. Cut and

fastened in a conch—confined

to the limits given (not her own)

a piece of (through a grid)

W... W... Wo...

a wide open mouth with no sound

.

She is gone—

Spread wide for idolaters:

Daughter of   'man'

sculptured, taken, chosen. Am I

suitably shaped to generate?

(*the sound of the land*) to create?

(*the sound*) Where can I find her?

EARTH

Behold Now, The Ground Beneath,

brings only   to the eyes of those

who   traveled   across   it

far   and   wide.

"Nothing will be retained from them,

which they have imagined to do."

Le premier mot   take the field   *Le premier bruit*

hold still   *Qu'el est la forme?*   hold the needle still

Qu'el est la ligne?   make the mark   *Qu'el est la phrase?*

even more painterly   *A la recherche d'un mot*   enter the hole

Cette contradiction   in a composition   *Le premier mot*

lines converge   *Le précipice?*   that very point

At the epigean divisions along racial, sexual, moralistic

and intellectual lines   a forest of factories   so that whatever

side we're on we stand stagnating   *Any little bit will do to pull*

the rest through   this clogged surface   *slide right in*

this cavity filled with noise   (exfoliated)   this lattice

of words   *Telement fragile*   this agitated landscape

(built by accretion)   this opening at the top

Qu'el est le mot?   that had once been so beautiful

We (the family group) were scattered abroad more than once
(a familiar labyrinth)   so we moved closer together
(the padlock fastened so that one couldn't breathe)   In the bowels
of the telluric, between highways and the proportions of time,
we remained motionless   we hid from the nightmare
(A book in which only certain chapters are read, others ignored)
How else can one live on the soft wet earth?   plotting objects in a
packed room   "Do not our lives consist of the four
elements?"   *Intruding on some intimacy*   "Faith,
so they say, but I think it rather consists of eating and drinking."
At the crossroads a counterpart is sung: One   the diaphragm
expands   Two   *Now is the hour*   Three
for the mouth   Four   to   open
Some   things   have   to   be   repeated

The soil around these grounds must first be tested before one can

begin building   (so the pieces will fit together in the end)   Soil,

in a period of physiologically enforced dormancy, cannot produce

brooks of water,   fountains that spring out from valleys and hills,

land that produces wheat and barley   The vine, the fig tree,

the pomegranate were frozen in a ditch   Olives and honey

trampled in an open field   The murmur of Arctic winds

a reminder of what had to be dug up   Our testimony

Our walled-in tragedy   Our new dwelling,

expelled from space and time   (soil being a living

organism ready to adapt and change at a moment's notice)

Our   clouded   space   expands   and   contracts

All parts are related to the whole   Look:

A word can be insuperable   Another, a tabernacle

One can be so careful that one can become a mere ghost   *Hunters*
are in the forest go in and wear red   or a handful of bones   *Devils*
are in the desert go in and bear yellow   The heart is taken out as if
it were a splinter, in one sweeping gesture   Our terrain trembled,
trampled by so many boots: left, left, left right left   "noises
in the darkness of the night"   left, left, left right left   "the groans
of the wounded"   left, left, left right left   "filled with
their cries"   left, left, left right left   What happened
once we left the cell though   is another story (the other
side of the window)   a book that tells the secret about
life in North America   which coast are you willing to enter?
Embedded in rock   One person's struggle illuminates the rest
Light kept trying to force itself in   *Hide in another name*
though I was practically blindfolded   *Hide deep inside*

A landscape can be viewed from any window   "An altar of stone"

frames the opening through which we see   (and moving it no easy

business)   its weight casts an anchor in a desert   (sand or snow)

or a jungle   (city or Amazonian)   "Brought forth into

this wilderness"   what is seen confined to what one wants to see

(some towers have no windows)   or the discovery sighted limited

to our particular imagination   We put a yoke around it

and demanded that it should serve us   no questions asked

Hardened and held in servitude   *then pulled back*   while a tough

musculature grew around my bowels   What seeds were planted?

the knot is tightened   Who made those abusive remarks?

sothatIcouldn'tfeel,   respondtomyownflesh,   tothehereandnow?

When our house dangled on a chain it was not related to the

praedial, so   we   heard   the   awful   screech   of   metal   links

To let the senses roam unfettered, unrestrained by pieces of furniture

But I am immured in this century like a fly in a bog,

a phrase fixated, repeated over and over   This grasping

at spongy ground,   poorly drained,   surrounded by sedges

(A little girl plays a board game)   Looking back at the last pages

(at where she had been)   I taste the salt which falls like pillars

down my cheeks   This touch   This is not what I had in mind

My *faiblesse*   the axis of how I happened

to perceive my earthly existence   *de femme*

Humbled by my predicament   (that of being thrown around,

for example,   lifted by his strength and finding myself landed

in the other room)   I decided to grow up   (before my time)

until I realized that my project had always been horizontal

" A n   a l i e n   i n   a   s t r a n g e   l a n d "

Who will lie with Him to preserve the seed of the father?

(And this question was asked with perfect seriousness)

To "lie with" involves many kinds of manipulation   (by hand,

foot, mouth, lips, penis, or eyes)   and the lover, if predisposed

to planting seeds, will walk down long corridors and rot in the soil

Any little bit will do to pull the rest through   "broken me asunder"

The material is measured and cut   "taken me by the neck and"

Sometimes a pattern is used   "shaken me to pieces"

I had to embark remembering   Rationality crawls into the

picture, points its finger and gives reasons for the "lying" that was

done hundreds of years back   *there are shaded regions*

She shakes bitterly   (light tremble from an outsider's perspective)

each   piece   has   to   be   stitched   together

(earthquakes   were   what   I   recall   to   mind)

In a roomful of people waiting for my marriage, what is generally remembered is that a struggle took place   hesitation confused the current   no clearing   (ask yourself how many of your thoughts are really your own)   a nation grows, sowed, scattered by the dead 'til it no longer has any memory but that which it was given   My feet were firmly planted (I thought) but an unconscious choice was made   surprised by pleasure one can begin to remember that one is not advancing or developing   a "quick" excavation will not give you "the bigger picture"   To observe means to see (a boulder must be removed from the window) things for what they really are   I kept forgetting things, ignoring others   The animal thrown in the cellar   I forgot to keep my senses alert to everything going on around me Until   there   was   nothing   left   but   sounds

I pick up stones one by one: sandstone, obsidian, shale, limestone

". . . all that power sweeping savagely in and inevitably withdrawing,

hypnotized, and the two senses of that vastness and this tininess . . ."

corundum, carnelian, granite   (It's important not to lose

one's notes, or the surface will grow hard and dry like the upper

layer of earth around a city)   I look at their shapes:

flat, banded, spherulitic, stratified, hexagonal   their textures:

smooth, lustrous, sedimentary, crystalline, sharp   *Une pierre*

S h e   f i n d s   p l a c e s   t o   h i d e   *U n   c a i l l o u*

The garden turns to stone until all the shit is washed off

"A word will never be able to comprehend the voice that utters it"

In a body of standing water   *Qu'el est le mot?*

my companions   as I rested

WATER

Flowing waters

rend   when bubbling

dissolve into the interior

of the earth

animate and divine

"I take it slow"

    Sometimes—

        "What if then *is* now?"

Whether flat or sharp

    I follow the notation

        or perhaps I portent

something else—a descent

    in broad daylight,

        from higher to lower,

if you believe in division,

    a desire for something

        more than an heirloom

at the quivering waterline

    More than my hesitation,

        this shudder at the shore

This meeting of mouths

       trapped with thirst,

              hinged at the surface

Wavering between then

       and now and the rooms that fit

              inside me like columns

Where is the door to this one

       or that one? I watch light

              steal under water

so that it ripples,

       so that snow will melt

              from previously forgotten

silenced or deadened parts

       of the body—the pull of the line,

              as fibers twist and coil

around the corner of my past

How can I know the present

if the swollen cry "Restrain"?

"Excessive!" "Demanding!" "Too . . . !"

Those tugs on the leash

that bled the engram,

that decimated the floorboards,

that filled the drawer with water

so that there wouldn't be enough

room remaining, or else flushed

down the pipes, the impurities

filtered, and a life force depleted

At the intersection of two

roads, be not bound by

cultivation, by exact

measurements; this kind of

    oblivion will cramp and fetter

        the spirit, this "fitting in"

What have we managed to

    change but the surface?

        Nuances. Words used to describe

"Too!" I hear an echo of it

    in my ear, a legacy

        passed on so that I was

split and divided—but I want to

    descend along the dense,

        animate river encircling the earth

I want to glide softly over

    the cold ocean like a Monarch

        butterfly, plunge into its opacity

But I am stopped short—

    gasping, grasping, barely

        a breath in all my . . .

A mort is heard in the

    distance—a killing is made

        in overwhelming quantities

Minnows balance themselves

    "and the sudden silent trout

        all lit up, hanging,

trembling"   Traveling

    in a felucca through

        a shade called "America"

A past cut in bone

    What's in a name?

        A cascade? An ideogram?

An emblem? And beneath it?

Dominion is devoid of light

Can't even swim across the moat

I forgot my watercolors

(flooded with memories of a

woman and man fighting over . . .)

The sound of the sea separates

the mainland and the island;

How could I paint a picture?

The tone wrestles with itself

along transparent waves,

feet immersed in sharp sand

Herself and myself—The Pacific crashes

and the threat of that wide open

beach, the imagined threat

Suddenly all breaks, splits—

As I drive from one side

to the other, a childhood drenched

"Now these are the generations of . . . "

To reduce the impact, I curl

my body forward

This passage backward marked

a meridian, nothing, nobody

would be the same after

Her body, my body,

succulents that encompass the

conflict, the divide,

On the way to that uncharted region,

the way of contradiction,

beyond the lighthouse

(if cast in an empty pit,

     a cavity with no water, remember the

          tears buried in past centuries—Now!)

That place, shelter of my imagination,

     out of reach, made of stones

          the size of my stomach

For no apparent reason will a

     child die in its first years—

          a narrow elided fishing line

The anonymous pass from view

     (Would that be too hard to take?)

          no light, and rapture thaws the body

and that changes everything

     the final state, this prolongation

          of vocal sounds

AIR

"The words (she was looking out

the window) sounded as if they

were floating like flowers."

and   she   vanished   into

air   drawn   lines

a   melody   in   strophic   form

The cold is fierce, the wind, the space available, made available

for the child, pierces walls, double windows, and numbs light.

The space available, made available, or unavailable, retracts;

a refuge withdrawn. Her air thins—her breath measured out.

"I cautious, scanned my little life—"

VAPOR   CANNOT   PAINT   A   PICTURE   CAN

I wondered if the heavens were

                    developing large gaps like holes in the ozone

In the late 20th century, the piercing question is: How much are we

willing to exchange for our share of space in the nebula?

In the late 20th century, phantoms in the guise of stellar wind

show her a faint tendency towards nothing. She is fissionable.

"Beware lest you lose the substance by grasping at shadows"

A   SWEET   FIRMAMENT   CHILD   A   SWEET

The aria began as a secret where I

                        was blamed for the part I played in the drama

The presence of seduction confuses the currents, breaks forth in the
atmosphere and affects everyone. The keeper of the prison is a wind.

The atmosphere affects everyone and she wonders if there will be
enough room for her thoughts to envelop a locality.

Words float on the page, sometimes a phrase, a line or a whole sentence

I   LANDED   IN   A   SOLITUDE   IN

Why is it so difficult for me to find

                              comfort in a volatile stream?

A genesis lasts a long time and is interpreted each according to the individual's

dream. If short of breath listen to gray hairs before they fall in the grave.

According to the dream she took too much space and had to retreat

in the chill currents of the narrow. This influence surrounds her.

"To give some form to the chaos inside me"

DENSE   DAY   DISSEMINATED

For now I see absence

                    darkly, before being painted over in layers of white

If famine follows "it shall be very grievous." A point on the compass. What came to pass caused a complete retreat of her memories into the past.

If famine follows it shall be a blow to the whole mass surrounding the earth, not just one child. Gas evaporates, but leaves a residue.

"The house we were born in is engraved within us"

SHARE   A   BRISK   BREAD

Attachment to crumbs

                              of information, that know only a part

Thinking of elements as well-defined personalities is perhaps a

mistake; it does not take in boundlessness and emptiness.

A mistake not to think of nothing as not, then we need pneumatic

devices to solidify abstractions, and it builds knots.

"Complete collapse. Lack of self-confidence. Aversion. Panic."

I   COULDN'T   I   ANYTHING   I

That hunger for the absolute must be crushed,

                    this grasping at the earth like a buoy in the ether

Whose blood is required so that we can fly over oceans? Refresh your

memory. She made herself strange, putting on airs, lost in brooding.

Whose blood is required? Her memories seek disclosure—confession.

Distress found her and she let it come.

"Every word born of an inner necessity"

A   DOUBLE   COULD   TRAVEL   A

It is difficult for us to understand

                    each other when we speak through interpreters

THE SPHERE

This is the region of those who hide,

who live buried in a harrowed landscape.

This is the terrain of those who disappear,

for whatever reason, who vanish, melt away.

This is the cenotaph, the crack in the tenor of certain

words, where a country eclipses its own people.

This is the domain of those flailing in the wind,

bounding off surfaces, the narrow regions of the apogee.

"We start transparent and then the cloud thickens.

All history backs our panes of glass."

At the edge of my own disappearance,

in the wake of elements that shaped my body,

I turned and noted the treasure that was left

behind in my sacks. I was shy at first,

a mere sliver of the little girl I had been,

afraid the compass would steer me in the wrong,

of exceeding the limits of what was appropriate,

for a "woman" I mean. What I remembered was

the imprecision of this inner life, and my efforts

left me murmuring. How many years were swallowed?

It is difficult to sing in face of the other.

What was audible? What could be distinguished?

Off the coast, cloaked in a reverie, anchored

in brine, on this almost-island, jutting out

My hand reached toward a word, a phrase—

a fragment in this auditorium of noise

where landing on the shoal was obscured

by the repetitive pronouncement that the propertied

were persons of more definite space,

of wide influence, not sediments disturbed.

The pillar I had become disintegrated,

the inconsolable features uncertain of having been

a gracious landscape, that terrain engraved

by my former state, the path of my past.

A sapling bows its head, soaked by wind.

I shake all over. A leaf hardly formed,

clinging to the groove on this branch,

the weight of it spread out upon her back.

I carry it, these cracks. Her wales. Her burdens.

I washed my flesh and refrained from exposing

the cloud which severed my mind from my body,

(rooted by a law rather than a choice to stand upright).

I had forgotten how to breathe, so that each gasp

came in hurried intervals, uttered the indiscernible.

Bending forward, charred,   blown up at the trunk,

a knot sown at the vista of my imagination.

Washed up on shore during high tide,

secreted on that narrow anatomical strip,

a cephalopod's "rage to order the words of the sea";

copulating with rocks, pebbles, and sand in my

hands—I dug deep into the voices of the past

until I reached a calcified internal shell, all

the pushing in the world couldn't get me past that grip.

Turning away from the bow, my legs about to give way,

to kneel on this raft made of sticks and foliage—

Oceans have softened boulders through centuries

if you know how to wait, bit by bit, line by line.

A sea traveler's past seen as no one dares to see it.

The dreamer asks that the woman's life be saved.

Those dying went ashore induced to pretend, to fake it,

the way plants are encouraged to grow indoors.

Who was willing to show how they were torn into pieces?

Arcane knowledge projected its commandments,

and the proper pause was expected before being taken.

I was grieved and angry to be sold to the void,

a slave to the opinion of others, a drop of blood in a toilet;

it put me underground when I was longing for birth.

"Being broken. Speaking broken."

My remains would be found elsewhere, in the aftermath

of a small bedchamber with purple pansies on the night table.

All I could do now was determine my own inner responses

and sterics detected something down there, south of my midriff.

In this globular body my intestines pulpy, shriveled,

weak—the pressure from other regions thrust open

a vulnerable unknown zone, a famished thirsty island,

a longing for something greater than myself.

I forgot that what I hoped for, and at the same time dreaded,

was being completely alone with a blank sheet of paper.

But there is none "whose inward being is so strong

that it is not greatly determined by what lies outside of it."

All holy texts are provisional (you do not see her yet),

stain that which is not possible to distinguish.

What I had learned was fear, to fear my own thoughts

my own dreams, my own visions, my own ambition—

the child I had been eclipsed by ideas and beliefs

so solid, so grounded that I became a somber shade

of what I had been, a weary, lusterless eye

sojourning in a foreign land threshed with guts.

My prayers had vanished with the lust

for fame—a storm at the center of the sphere—

and I became a globule of self-restraint

no longer astonished or agitated by the vitality of color.

Extinction happens only to a rare species—

A fade out on the Scribe.

The

perforated

map

Text is set in 10 point New Baskerville.

Printed in an edition of 600.